FEBRUARY TOAST

WILLIAM P. MOORE

Designed/Published by WPM Productions
Hollywood, FL
Distributed by Lulu Press
Photos and title page artwork by the author.

William P. Moore
"February Toast"
Printed in the United States of America
First Printing: April 2014

ISBN 978-1-304-98068-7

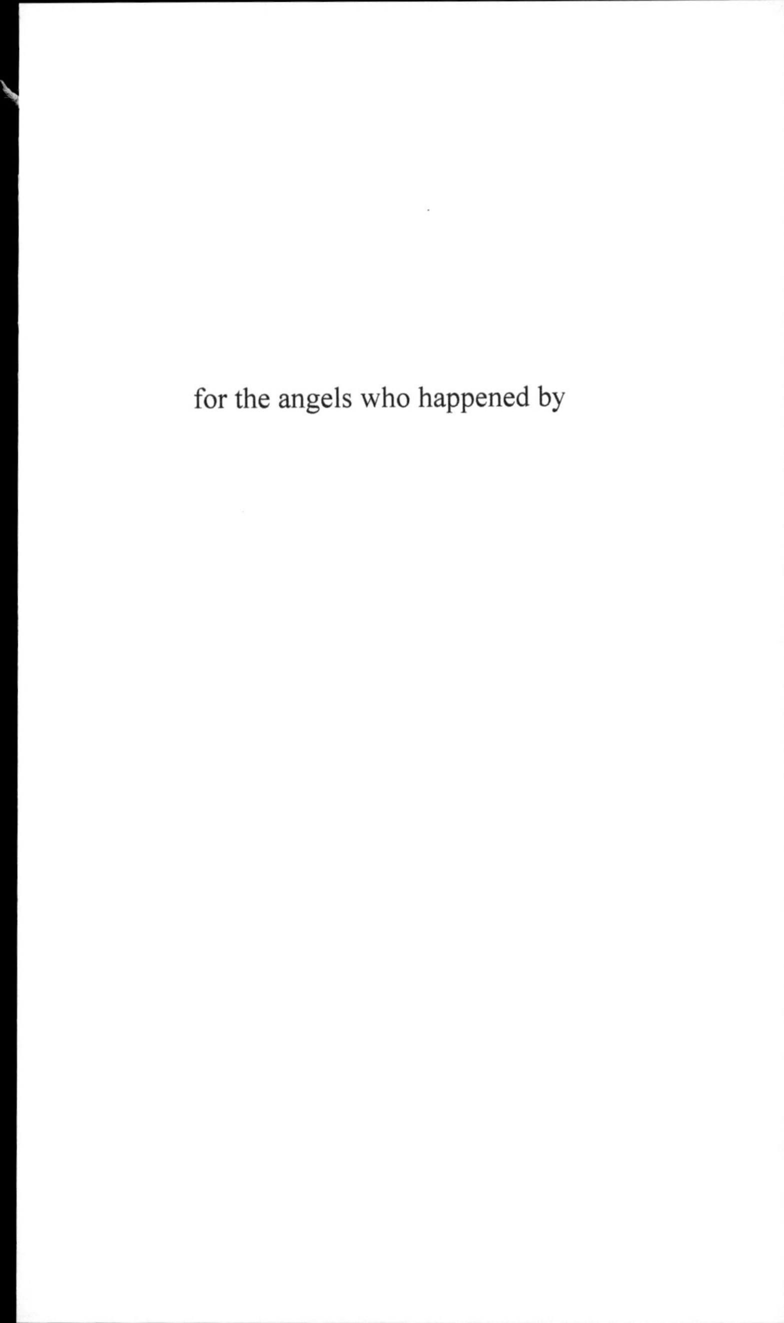

for the angels who happened by

“The art
of
the
short hair
is that
it
don’t
go on
for
too long.”

– Norman Mailer

CONTENTS

FEBRUARY TOAST

Pip pip cheerio and saludos cheers –
Let's drink to ancient presidents
and torturous valentines,
moving trucks and red red wines –
snowstorms on Sunday, flesh in the tropics,
neighbors we hate, incomplete biopics,
Atlantic-striped ties stained by nicotine,
bluesy friends whacked on Benzedrine,
boys soaked in hormones with guises and roles,
girls cloaked in perfume, spongy dark souls.

Bang one down for month two.
Within its four hazardous weeks
before the lion wheezes and creaks,
all left sane will likely go mad
Locked in cabins, no relief to be had.
Boric acid dusts the countertops and unknown
germs from generations past form a crust
like cancer in the gas cap stove.

We will try free verse with carriage returns
Fading like this – as our memory burns
Laughing hee hee at the wiki watchee
snacks on our knee, worshippin' tee vee.

Whoop whoop and down the hatch –
Here's to dinosaurs ever thirsty in museums,
to randy sailors and plump manatees,
to untended graves, the frigid north breeze.

The Joads drink gin on freeway exits,
Elephants stampede an invisible nexus.
The sirens of fate sing a bitter bolero,
while demons dance al contrario;
Between the poles of the morally upright
Lovers speak their clever lies at night.

Blinky winky mix me a stinky –
Another round for tavernous ghosts
Mythical heartthrobs and misguided boasts,
Black leggings over soiled pink lace
Reproduction rehearsals of the human race.

Wise are the beaten the noble the dying,
Into our beers lost chances go sighing,
By our breath and brain we're fogged,
Our Feb 1 pipe is frozen and clogged.

Cold bad luck and electrostatic hugs,
tyrant landlords, someone else's bugs,
Bad trombone, influenza, and wat'ry stew,
Roll a joint doobie doo,
Get us past this month, please hurry too.

MISSING THE MUSE

In the time of the milky white sky
She left, he doesn't know why.
She fled with the juice
Leaving his output obtuse
And dry the font of his writing supply.

He felt the wall of cinder white brick,
His spirits dulled by shovel and pick.
What once she brought daily as news
He found not at all, only fossils and clues
Marked with chalk and a keyboard click.

Then certain chemicals were tried
And foods consumed, fatty and fried.
Until reason ruled and calories measured
so pounds and words'r trimmed not treasured.
"Self denial's the path," a guru cried.

Yet blankness prevailed, and a winter coat
Killed the words he wrote.
Craggy yard, shaggy hair, shoes too loose,
A sea of Bordeaux the path of excuse,
He cast a bottle into a sea remote:
"Return, o muse to me," he quote.

COTTON

Travel the world and burn out your senses five,
that's what the old man did for years:
he spent it taking in the grandeur
then reached a fragile point where we exist
  before tipping,
like a Beechcraft over the bay with spent tanks.

His senses rebounded in the last year,
His nose worked again, best he ever smelt,
And the visions and memories that came along
were cut trees rushing downriver;

Splashes of women and bourbon
dwelt on over a plate of pretzels
and a wedge of sturdy cheese.
War and service and passenger props
seen in memory's sky above Macchu Picchu.

He could no longer grip the slipping time.
Inside green walls at road's end
he put on a soft cotton shirt,
which blocked the institutional chill
and wrapped him in private dream.
It felt damn fine, he told the ceiling,
like soft March air in Belize.

THE WHITE BLISS OF GORDON'S

We shouldn't be hard on her -
Hell she raised us, gave us everything
until we grew up and left her
and then she left us, in the most splitting way.

Isolated summer days by the swamp
one after another hearing the bamboo grow.
She's spine-slumped on the couch
surrounded by the stale smell of daytime TV.
She's sedentary yet restless,
her legs jangly with fouled energies
looking forward to when her pal Mimi calls,
the ringing recognizable and regular;

They commiserate over heavy plastic phones
with highballs and goofballs.
Plot developments on *Search for Tomorrow*
Tossed around by quite a different staff.

One day a week with duty more than will
she dresses for the store,
all those clothes to choose from
for 30 minutes at the A&P.

Or sometimes it's to Max's Deli
or Sunny's dry cleaners

and if breathing the air liberates her enough,
even a stop for curb-service lunch:
a barbecue with slice of purple onion
and a dill pickle wedge, alone in the Buick.

By sunset she's house-robe numb from
the white bliss of Gordon's,
meaning supper will burn
like a chunk of dead meat
and boys and cats will sulk unfed
and the old man will fume at wit's end
in heavy mum retreat
to his workbench seat.

No one knew
what to do
back then.

So we shouldn't be hard on her -
Hell she raised us, gave us everything
until we grew up and left her
and then she left us, in the most splitting way.

PAGEANTRY AT NATURAL BRIDGE

A little girl circa 1958
threw up in the dining room
at Natural Bridge Inn, Virginia.
She had the fish; we could smell it.
We stared at chuck wagon steaks
on our sad green plates
and ate slowly, not too hungry,
while a janitor mopped up
and the flounder in the air
became ammonia in the air

Replaced by smoke in the air
from dad's cigarette as we went outside
to little walls where people sit and
we sat dutifully in the dark
then the show began with Sousa
or maybe How Great Thou Art – what's the diff,
While a narrative droned with colored lights that
violated the night of the mighty stone arch
While a rushing creek spilled past black rocks,
Its sounds the holy unmentioned souls of yore,
Whispering beneath the amplified narrative.

The night air smelled of corn
as the speaker droned verses of Genesis

and I had to assume He who made the pretty
bridge and the little girl
made the bad fish too.

With mercy the show ended
brighter lights came, scouts emerged, saying
"All praise the Park Ranger, okay?"
And amid scraping metal chairs,
"Don't forget the donations box."

An interview for her opinion twenty years after, a
grown gal returns, Miss Bridge
who now eats carrot sticks
on vacation from her TV show and
asked about the pageant, says in a sultry way:

"I believe the show you know and the waters
rushing by the stone cutaway like you know, ad-
dress our national diversity and so forth,
like the colored lights and so forth, as well as the
hymns and reciteyfications you know
and so forth that make it all special, so to speak."

SEEMINGLY

To say it seems, say *parece que*
followed by explanations and excuses

and then the contradictions
and then the isolation
and the empty park
of memories and fantasies followed by
the condemnations and libations
the frustrations and complications.

Then disregard it, after all,
because
parece que does not translate to say it is
but seems.

DWINDLING

They went somewhere but they are not sure
where; they thought of it and then forgot.
Something is dwindling and whether or not
it's their attention or the object of it
no one can say, that is to say
no one could hear them explain one way or an-
other because they aren't there anymore.

THE NEWS IS FREAK

1959
A globe spins, an overture plays,
Before the ads for pain and malaise.
Plain folk who watch tonight
And aren't feeling well might
Injure their spleen and cry you're mean
At John Cameron Swayze
Whose Windsor's gone crazy

Tieless Leonard Bernstein lectures
the kids on oboes and strings and
draws in a notebook all the things
that give imagination its wings.

At station break, bits of Bufferin move
in an idiot diagram past digestive valves,
racing bowel-ward in a cartoon gut.

Next, Porter Wagoner will ask Dolly
To sing of laxatives by golly
Out there in TV Land
Where the news is freak
eight days a week.

JOTTED DOWN

Man on a rooftop shouted
I wish I'd taken better notes.
I want it on my tombstone:
Next time I'll take better notes.

What's the big deal about better notes? someone
asked.
And by the way get your ass down from there.
Are the notes that you did take so bad?
Or not enough?
Would better notes account for this Mystery?
Would they assure a more comprehensible trip
next time around?

Man came down and
said, I'm telling you eye to eye
I could have used them.
Notes are historic, he continued,
Notes are understanding.
Notes are part of the calling to write.
The best by far are handwritten,
jotted down.

Well, I don't know if all that's true, someone
growled.

It is. So many years escaped unwritten.
Didn't say wasted!
More like allowed to get away.

whispering:
Yes allowed to get away,
That's easy to see, isn't it?

TOUR BUS ROUTES

Danger Boulevard
Misguided Avenue
Putrid Street
Intestinal Loop
Libido Lane
Morbid Mall
South Dumbfuck Highway
High Expectations Terrace
Gastro Beltway
Adrenalin Drive
Vicious Circle
Pathological Parkway
Chickenleg Road
Wart Court
Trapdoor Turnpike
Calle Frígida

ANT DEATH

They ate the bait until gorged, then emitted
a mumbly inebriated sort of ant talk,
returning home under suspicion
with poison jelly eyes met by ant doubts;
Some were diverted yet enough of them reached
the inner chambers of the bored queen
who fed on their toxins in an endless dinner
fueling herself like an idling jet liner
attended by workers and pruners
all of whom released a microaudible ant groan
prior to their soldierly ant demise
leaving robust queenie helpless
to wither incapable alone.
Outside eternity keeps humming,
the day goes by
despite her repeated signals, her black box.

HELSINKA

Helsinka O'Chevski appears in night dreams,
elusive yet filled with abandon.
Helsinka O'Chevski breaks hearts when she's
seen,
and makes her lovers sleep late in futile pursuit.
Helsinka O'Chevski in the light of day
was provisional and ciphered her angles.
Helsinka O'Chevski was being Googled long
before there was a Google.
Helsinka O'Chevski could beat the band and
pick a pocket then slip away fast.
Helsinka O'Chevski could be leading edge
trendy or old world simple
and was best at either extreme;
Helsinka O'Chevski is gone but the radio still
plays her. Another's dream is her screen.

NO CONSEQUENCE

The raptors are busy in lowering skies;
People keep their small pets inside;
An English sparrow (quietly touring South
Florida)
pecks at bugs on lawn's edge with no posture of
fear

then ups and flies zip zig zag away when a car
pulls in;
It's the girls from El Salvador with their buckets
and Kirby
coming for a rapid pre-holidays clean. I go out
back
and load up the feeder with raw peanuts for the
bluejays
who clink and clank and fuss at cat

who follows while I brush pool algae
then cat sips pool water in a kneel from the
coping like a wild animal
daring any red tail or white falcon to swoop,
though once ago, aforesaid cat as kitten
hid this time of year in no-bird-entry places
and chattered at sky birds strange
signals of no consequence.

HAMBURGER HEROES

Heroes change the world. They move it ahead a notch.

Accomplishments by a real hero have the power to alter the way we treat each other and what we believe at the core.

A hero can lift us up so our individual lives change. Usually much more than we realize.

The advent of a hero, like the tread of a giant, can really shake things up.

Accustomed creatures as we are, we are leery of tectonic shifts in our culture.
But heroes cannot be denied.

When a hero is stomping around, there are presentiments waiting to be discovered.
Signals of action and reaction.
It is important that we pay attention.

Consider examples of a hero of choice.
Then factor that hero's deeds by a thousand.
That's the hero we all need.

Think about it while you have the best possible cheeseburger in your own anxious hometown.

SONG OF THE STRANGE ROOM

Things are just like other things
in Metaphor City.

The saloon serves up medicine
to visitors, who say hey

This place is a lot like Simile Island
just off the coast of the Specific Ocean.

MOTORBIKER W/ A GIRL PROBLEM

He used her, the plain little Nurse passing by who let him kiss her right out there in the street as if they were lovers so the little act would invoke jealousy in the Chronic Girl (C.G.) who stood right beside them in a competitive stance. C.G. was twenty-two and all body business and not the brainiest type.

Never seemed he could he shake her and so he thought coming on to the unknown Nurse was a good gambit, so good maybe it would be like a last straw: Like sorry C.G. We're done, you *comprende*?

Earlier Chronic Girl woke up compound instead of simple. First thing, she tried to burn his motorbike house down using a stolen welder's kit. Her operator errors prevented disaster.

The motorbiker rumbled into a book fair, where inside was a big tent air-conditioned. People came in and out for a breather from the heat.

The motorbiker talked with a redhead a Mizz Strawberry who sold romance novels and didn't object to advances.

Even hotter day, at a water park party. High on the platform before the descending plastic rapids, a beam of sunlight displayed Chronic Girl's pocked skin that wrapped the corruption and promiscuity steaming in her blood.

Complementing her white one-piece was a pool float around her waist, which acted like her bumper for personal space when anyone squished and squeaked against it, unable to advance.

Motorbiker a tough guy in line at the water-slide, all boss in his black trunks and wet black hair, and at his hip was Mizz Strawberry in white porcelain skin speckled by cosmic moles, red copper wet locks extending from beneath a pale yellow bucket hat, jealously invoking…

…Chronic Girl who atop aforesaid water-slide ready to launch, her elegant and sleek frame wrapped in a blow-up dragon, reached back in the line and seized motorbiker's ankle to pull him down in the contra-current where she was hoping he could get a lesson or maybe even drown.

VIGNETTE OF JANE THE FLIGHT ATTENDANT

I'm doing procedural things late at night in the dim yellow of the forward galley. It's not soundproofed. No carpets. Lots of kitchenware, metal and plastic.

In the old days they wore heels in here. Clacked around. No longer. Elegance lost in a world of foam rubber soles.

Suicidal sister was on my mind. Turns out the all-Amerikan girl was a sweet con. Sis put her legs in the air, earning her way up to status and money and then took a guy twenty years younger, someone like an office mailroom boy, with the reliable equipment she craved. Married him. Got a place by the lake, a boat, extra places to live. Conspired profits. Laundered money from bad sources. Escalating fucked-up-ness.

It was all *muy extravagante* and shady. The law came eventually.

That was my sister Andrea. Annie. Everyone adored Annie, a real shrewd homecoming queen. Had her babies before 21 and by forty was hell on wheels, super-pretty super-bitch looking out for *número uno*. Ándrea became Andréa. The lingerie changed. Went first-name basis with the local cosmetic surgeon. The DA called one evening via detectives in the foyer. Grand jury next. She battled until her money and luck ran out, then fled to Ireland but disliked it and one foggy day said fuck extradition immunity anyway and jumped off a mountain.

I am her younger sister Jane. You may have run into me at the best places in New York. Or in a bar in Mexico. A cafe in Zurich or on the dance floor in Ibiza.

Hey, I never hang out in Nowheresville.

OCUPADO sign goes on and off to my left. With the throw of a bolt. My agenda and my heart.

Pot of burned coarse-grind clicks off, still aromatic. The red light replacing the green. Below there are the usual rattles and flight-noises from the array of warming lockers, a comforting harmonic. The tray ovens are STRAC and lined up hup-two, empty since the bankruptcy.

A bilingual dictionary is on the small formica counter, wrinkled from use and page-stained.

Lance found a bug in an oven earlier during the first-class cookie bake. He squealed. He does that. It's funny to see a uniformed man freak out. We have pills and free mini-bottles to help all types.

Our engines changed pitch. We're in the pattern. I notice the view changes in the door porthole. I can see buildings, grids and blocks, and vast plains of lights. The view extends farther when the pilot banks, showing off this sentimental sight of Amerika after dark.

The smell of our cabin air changes
from pressurized to real.
The permeated odors of coffee and first-class chocolate chip cookies go away, and I begin to imagine I can smell the people. Like canvas sneakers and overworked talc.

I grab the mike for a routine blurb,
hesitant to step even two paces outside
the warm galley,
my Somewheresville.

CONFUSED VISIONS OF DIAMOND

Forget the plea under the pergola,
the confused visions of diamond.
You already have one? Zayre's?
How about a real one?

(Never covet lest ye die boy,
a code shunned
in the rip current of attraction,
but worst offense
was to presume replacement)

Wines of seaweed and tidal surf,
maps drawn by Byronic heroes,
the halls of Ravel and Stravinsky,
high voltage storm, the element follows them
into unseen corner tables in bars,
around corners of office buildings
near emergency generators

Snuck away and undercover again
she with her statue figure of a siren and
her sweet lime sherbet dripping
in the heat of midday in a Texas
rental of desire where urgent windows breathe
aroma of nearby olive oil cooking,
and insects hum in the pecan trees.

Oh do then and yet wait but do.
Not done, they go again a squeaky chair.

Apart there are psychic calls from lonely shores,
toe-writing in wet sand like SOS of Love
meanwhile wrecked inlets of broken fantasy run
under star struck delusions that aren't,
and red envelopes bring warnings

Slow burn of cheap table wine
no more underwear tossed
on a frivolous lampshade
instead the tarot and arcana,
its cards solemn on the carpet.
Stopped. Dead end ahead.
Those are cards and they are too.

Drop off the key, Noveaux Frenchy,
Goodnight Irene, Happy Halloween.

SOBRECARGADO

La única parte buena de la sobrecarga es cuando se reduce la carga.

The only good part of being overloaded is when the load lightens.

HARDSCAPE

Part of that means concrete, wet cement, side-
walks and nouveaux terrazzo, putty putty mixer,
the whole nine yards, driveways with stakes and
red flags; slosh it out, discrete patch with palm
print, date and sign, X+Z, heart/

It comes from desolate factories with sand heaps
and storage towers that lurk with modest logos
like Cemex, a Mexican concern gone global, a
huge player as the world hardscapes itself/

These outposts for dispensation are nestled
among hills of sand dug out from Florida substra-
ta and dispensed with formula and water into
chunky trucks with huge gray tires like elephants.
They dump their chutes at excited sites and reload
at depressed ramps/

Like the one in old Rosemont circa 1987 when
one night a crazed tech writer I knew, a NASA
layoff casualty, shot a .38 pistol from his apart-
ment balcony, drunk, trying to kill the high tower
at the concrete plant across the tracks where a
featureless structure blinked red in the night and
reflected his lonely and frustrated existence that
he wanted also to end/

SOCIAL NETWORK PRAYER RAP

God spare us Mugbook and ratchet-jaw Twitter
All that stuff's going straight in the shitter.

Grant us real writing
in the weblog smog, where
the language will radiate and imaginate,
pontificate and metaphoriate –

Seems to me at sixty-three
Tweetin's got no arts,
just me-me dope from mundane charts,
benign and fine for those who like that line,

but to me at sixty-three
that table talk chatter
lacks substance and matter –
no muse no call just flung spitball.

So bury me not on the Mugbook wall,
I prefer my lot on lonely blogspot:

Land of the blog, dog,
Blessed is the blog, dog;
Blessed is the blog.

REJECT THE CANDIDATE

Brush your teeth with radishes boys,
Belinsky's coming, I dread.
Keep him far away boys,
Blink not, breathe back the dead.

Belinsky's hideous lies
are not disguised
by his rich man ties.

Only the loco believe this Bobo.

Tonight we seal things tight
When Belinsky's in our face, alright?

MAGIC REALISM AT THE BOOKSTORE

Speaking to electric tablet, live blogging:

The complete poems of Robert Service just burst
into flames.

Tristram Shandy unveiled his Facebook page.

The Bronte Sisters are shooting Instagrams to
Rick and Don Barthelme.

All 1,500 of the Writers Digest how-to-publish
books turned into wolverines and gnawed at each
other until Reference was a bloody crime scene.

At which point Elmore Leonard left the store,
tallboy beer and cigarette in hand, meeting up
with Hunter T and fifth of Bacardi Silver.

Joyce lost in Land of Hyperlinks,
Twain is tweeting.

Oprah came in to hawk her Nooks
and Doctor Phil shot selfies in Modern Health

exposing his Mister Fort Worth
and was hauled away by brave Ulysses.

A trio levitated above the mystery section:
Chandler, MacDonald, and Hammett.
They waved:
Come back again, dammit.

FIRST-BASE BEAUTY

Back then she wore tall leather boots and
a tee shirt to bed.
She made allusions to Bleak House
as he roamed the bountiful landscape
under her Princeton emblem;
Down below near her wedge of nylon pink
she blocked and stopped him cold
and boot-kicked his leg and said
Don't go there dude -

What a first-base beauty she was,
said same guy with three-day beard
overgrown into gray
over a cracked hardboiled egg
peeled on the sink's edge
by the newspaper on the counter
by a bottle of ale
forty years later
reading her obituary.

MOON CONCEITS

She wanted the gleam of a cold star
To chase its eager contrail
To submit and be conquered
Rather than indulge the warm gravity
And mellow light of a lazy moon.

On departing he realized
She wasn't the universe,
only a brief solar flare.

The moon's a ping-pong ball, he said
on your side of the net every 28 days.
    ping . . . pong.

Or depending
per mood and mindset
a button on a Cuban silk shirt,
a slice of cantaloupe
an ice-coated nickel
a desert bone
a cheese ball
a toe nail
an orange lozenge
a grapefruit rind
a single headlight
a surfcaster's beacon in a fish's eye –

On shore rum drinks blend by tidal pull.
The head-stricken reach for saturated Anacin,
the tablet a daylight moon dissolving
in a damp sink.

After dark the detergent moon whitens
Love Boulevard
bleaching the follies
and disguising the stains.

Indian summer moon lights on barracks;
No satisfaction, a radio plays
from study lamp yellow windows
into an old Richmond pine grove,
insects and adult lives just beginning.

Gal's cornbread like soft and warm yet
can get crusty and hard fast, mean and crumbly
And she can turn away and put you out
on a midnight driveway whoosh just like that
to shiver new and alone with loss and sudden
nausea under a farmhouse blue moon.

Or it can beam on snow in unmatched display
Making an illusory white lightning blanket
All from that ball in space, that moment's gleam
between the trees or on the pond that
same light which showcased pyramids.

CAVALIER CLUB

Where once a round nightclub platform
extended onto the wide beach, a fanciful Gatsby
site with colorful awnings and snazzy bunting,
café tables and a parquet floor above sand /

Same sand where a metal detector and shovels
seek pocket change, old dimes maybe, or a GI
watch, or even a gold ring slung seaward
during a spat while Dorsey played

As war couples danced on summer nights;
some took to cabanas for drinks and a tryst
in sanctified spaces under the submarine towers
drab sentinels with tiny rectangle eyes
half shuttered like theirs against the sea breeze

While behind them inland, unseen,
Edgar Cayce's ghost haunted the odd hill
not far from the Hotel, tall, grand and colonial
Where years ago someone jumped from the spire
they say, after a devastating day
in the Market.

SIX NIGHTS OF WITCH

Anxiety on the opposing shore of a flooded lake
where voices drone in corporate speak
across the still water:
na-NIYA, ni-NUGA, guh-NERK.

Energy fields of dreadful propositions,
fear of navigating the darkened room
after pitch-black invasions
the second month of the year
by mean ass witches who for six nights
accordant to the evil clarity of
their scripted witch dreams
bring torment.

Urging another dimension,
luring, their hooks catch muscles of heart;
scheming under rainy magnolias
the dark ones laugh,
expert mistresses of derision.

Plain late
clothes wrong, shoes off, heart thumps
inch toward the dry camp where bullies
commemorate and take kudos or lumps
with gun holsters and god causes and
money troubles brewing on leap year 29th

Best take shelter with British gin
February's drink of choice
and hear some soothing music therein
Let the sedan cool in the carport,
Enter the house of mortgage and tax
Fret overgrown weeds, perilous trees.
Spray the baseboards, lock the gates,
get to your sock feet and step on crumbs,
smile in a sardonic way.

Drink the gin with a speared radish
or moon cut of fragrant lime,
push up your traveled sleeves
and let go

Dream and defend and
seek language art on a Chiclet keyboard
Hit return a lot, again
and again
so much so
and artfully so,
that day seven and March arrive
and a passing angel
displaces aforesaid witch haunts.

Till that happens,
Wait for the allies,
wait.

ABOUT THE AUTHOR

William P. Moore's books include *The Toluca Crime Report & Other Stories, Oceanaire, Houston Chemical, Fantastic Response, Tales of Don Pedro, and Dining with Hemingway. He is from Virginia and lives in South Florida.*

www.ingramcontent.com/pod-product-compliance
Ingram Content Group UK Ltd.
Pitfield, Milton Keynes, MK11 3LW, UK
UKHW020216250726
13967UKWH00001B/30

9 781304 980687